A NOTE TO PARENTS ABOUT BEING SELFISH

Mine! is a key word in most young children's vocabulary. And abandoning selfishness is often the most difficult step from early childhood egocentricity toward socialization. Therefore, it is not surprising that many parents have a hard time getting their children to share.

The purpose of this book is to teach children the importance and benefits of unselfishness. In addition, it provides practical ways for children to share their things.

Reading and discussing this book with your child will help him or her grow from a self-centered, selfish person into an others-oriented, unselfish one. In addition, it will help your child understand the true meaning of the words, "It is more blessed to give than to receive."

Even though sharing can be good for everyone involved, it is not necessary, or even appropriate, for children to share everything they possess. Indeed, sometimes it does not benefit anyone for something to be shared. It is important for your child and you to determine what constitutes situations in which sharing is inappropriate. Then, it is important for you to support your child's "selfishness" in these situations just as much as you support his or her unselfishness in other situations.

This book belongs to:

_____

Published by Scholastic Inc.
90 Old Sherman Turnpike, Danbury, CT 06816.

SCHOLASTIC and associated logos are trademarks and/or
registered trademarks of Scholastic Inc.

ISBN 0-7172-8579-0

First Scholastic Printing, September 2005

A Book About
Being Selfish

by **Joy Berry**

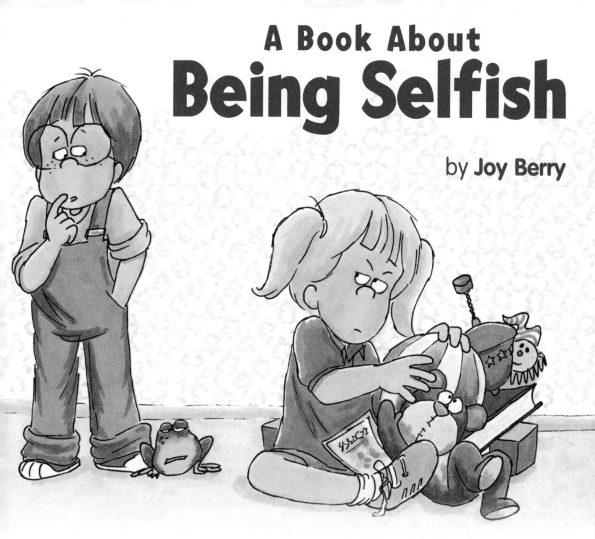

SCHOLASTIC INC.

New York   Toronto   London   Auckland   Sydney
Mexico City   New Delhi   Hong Kong   Buenos Aires

This book is about Katie and her friend, Sam.

Reading about Katie and Sam can help you understand and deal with **being selfish.**

Have you ever been with people who would not share their food with you?

Have you ever played with people who would not share their toys with you?

People who do not share are selfish.

They care more about themselves than about others.

When you are with someone who is selfish:
- How do you feel?
- What do you think?
- What do you do?

When you are with someone who is selfish:
- You might feel left out, frustrated, and angry.
- You might not want to be with that person.

It is important to treat others the way you want to be treated.

If you want others to share with you, you need to share with them.

You need to be unselfish.

Being unselfish does not mean that you have to share all your things all the time.

Sometimes you cannot share.

Put the food away if you do not have enough to share.

Try not to eat in front of someone who does not have anything to eat.

Try to be fair if you are going to share. Here is a good rule for dividing something:
- Let one person divide.
- Let the other person choose.

You might not want to share something that is special to you.

Do not use the special thing in front of someone else unless:

- The person does not want to use it.
- The person has something else to use.

You do not have to share with anyone who is careless.

Put your things away if you think they might be lost or damaged.

You can help other people take care of the things you share with them by doing these things:
- Show them how your things work.
- Show them how to take care of your things.

Be fair if there is only one of something that must be shared by two or more people.

- Take turns using it.
- Let each person use it for an equal length of time. You can use a clock or timer to help keep track of the time.

If you want to be happy, you should treat other people the way you want to be treated.

This means you should not be selfish because you do not want other people around you to be selfish.